01/08

Africa

MEL FRIEDMAN

Children's Press®
An Imprint of Scholastic Inc.
New York   Toronto   London   Auckland   Sydney
Mexico City   New Delhi   Hong Kong
Danbury, Connecticut

Content Consultant

Lily Saint
Graduate Center
City University of New York
New York, NY

Library of Congress Cataloging-in-Publication Data

Friedman, Mel.
 Africa / by Mel Friedman.
     p. cm. -- (A true book)
 Includes bibliographical references and index.
     ISBN-13: 978-0-531-16863-9 (lib. bdg.)
                 978-0-531-21825-9 (pbk.)
     ISBN-10: 0-531-16863-8 (lib. bdg.)
                 0-531-21825-2 (pbk.)

 1. Africa--Juvenile literature. I. Title.

 DT3.F75 2008
 960--dc22   2007048086

Produced by Weldon Owen Education Inc.

1 2 3 4 5 6 7 8 9 10 R 18 17 16 15 14 13 12 11 10 09

Find the Truth!

Everything you are about to read is true *except* for one of the sentences on this page.

Which one is **TRUE**?

T or F   The Nile is the longest river in the world.

T or F   A camel must eat twice a day.

Find the answers in this book.

Contents

THE **BIG** TRUTH!

Sounds of a Land

The Dogon of West Africa are known for their carved masks.

Sometimes sand dunes in the Sahara make a booming noise. Scientists believe it is the sound of sand grains colliding during a dune avalanche.

CHAPTER 1

Snapshot of a Continent

Africa is a place of diverse landscapes, peoples, and wildlife. It has mighty rivers and ice-capped mountains. It has scorching deserts and misty rain forests. As on other continents, people's lives have been affected by both natural and human-made events. Africa is the second-largest continent. Only Asia is bigger.

Winds whipping across the Sahara produce more than half the airborne dust in the world.

Baobab (BAOW-bab) trees store water in their thick trunks. They are sometimes called upside-down trees because they look as if their roots are at the top.

Hot or Very Hot?

In most of Africa, the climate is either hot and dry or hot and wet. Desert and **savanna** take up most of the land. In these areas, rainfall is rare or seasonal. Tropical rain forest covers much of the center of the continent. This region, close to the **equator,** has the wettest parts of Africa. The rainy season there lasts all year!

Africa

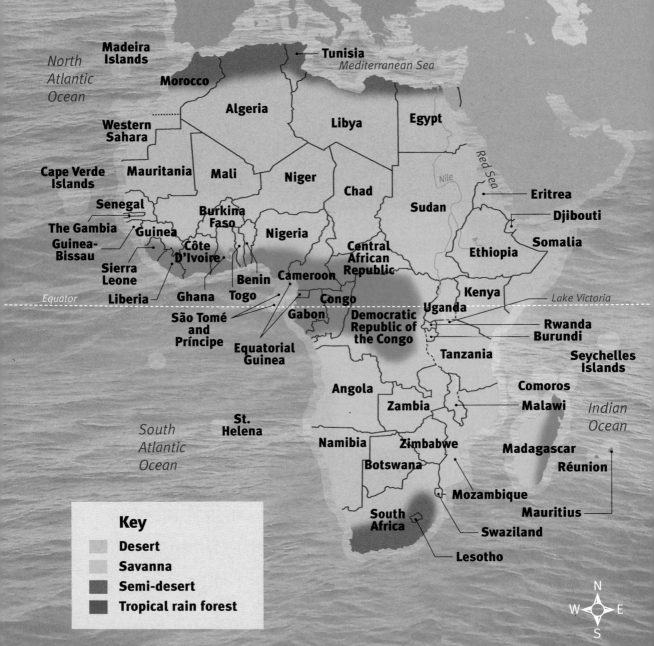

North Atlantic Ocean

Madeira Islands

Tunisia

Mediterranean Sea

Morocco

Algeria

Libya

Egypt

Western Sahara

Nile

Red Sea

Cape Verde Islands

Mauritania

Mali

Niger

Chad

Sudan

Eritrea

Djibouti

Senegal

Burkina Faso

Somalia

The Gambia

Guinea

Nigeria

Central African Republic

Ethiopia

Guinea-Bissau

Côte D'Ivoire

Sierra Leone

Benin

Cameroon

Kenya

Lake Victoria

Equator

Liberia

Ghana

Togo

Congo

Uganda

São Tomé and Príncipe

Gabon

Democratic Republic of the Congo

Rwanda

Burundi

Equatorial Guinea

Tanzania

Seychelles Islands

Angola

Comoros

Zambia

Malawi

Indian Ocean

South Atlantic Ocean

St. Helena

Namibia

Zimbabwe

Madagascar

Réunion

Botswana

Mozambique

Mauritius

South Africa

Swaziland

Lesotho

Key

- Desert
- Savanna
- Semi-desert
- Tropical rain forest

N W E S

9

Although the Sahara has huge areas of sand, most of it is actually rocks and gravel.

Dramatic Deserts

North Africa is almost completely taken up by the Sahara desert. Central and southern Africa have smaller deserts. In the deserts, there is almost no rain, and the air is very dry.

The Sahara is the largest and hottest desert in the world. It is about as big as the United States. Three thousand years ago, the Sahara was grassland. People grazed their animals on it.

River of Life

The Nile is the world's longest river, flowing for 4,160 miles (6,695 kilometers) from Lake Victoria to the Mediterranean Sea. It passes through nine countries, and supplies water to 300 million people.

In the past, the Nile flooded the fields of Egypt every year. The water made the land productive. Without the Nile, the civilization of ancient Egypt couldn't have developed. Today, dams control the flooding so that crops can be **irrigated** during the dry season.

The shadoof was the first mechanical method of irrigation. It was invented about 3,500 years ago, possibly by the Egyptians. It works like a seesaw. A weight at one end of a pole helps lift a filled bucket of water at the other end. Shadoofs are still used today.

Shadoof

Weight

Bucket

Madagascar has large areas of rain forest. Many unique species of plants and animals are found there.

Misty Rain Forests

The African rain forest is dense and dark. Tall trees crowd so closely together that their tops touch to form a leafy umbrella. The rain forest is home to many different kinds of animals. Some spend most of their time in the treetops, or forest canopy. Others are best suited to life on the forest floor. The forest layers combine to form a complex **ecosystem**.

Ice-Topped Mountains

There are only a few mountain ranges in Africa. The longest range is the Atlas Mountains. It is nearly 1,500 miles (2,414 kilometers) long. It lies at the northern edge of the Sahara, in Morocco, Algeria, and Tunisia.

Africa's highest peaks are volcanic. Mount Kilimanjaro is Africa's tallest mountain. It is 19,341 feet (5,895 meters) high, and is a **dormant** volcano. Although the mountain lies near the equator, its summit is always covered with snow.

At the base of Mount Kilimanjaro are dry grasslands. On the mountain, there are rain forests as well as permanent glaciers.

Every year, zebras, gazelles, and wildebeest travel about 1,000 miles (1,600 kilometers) across the savanna. They follow the rains to graze on new grass.

CHAPTER 2

Amazing Animals

Africa is one of the few places where large herds of animals still roam free. Many of the animals, such as giraffes and zebras, are found in the wild only in Africa. Scarce water, competition for food, and the threat of predators make survival a daily challenge for many African animals.

A zebra's stripes are like fingerprints. Each zebra has a unique pattern.

In the Rain Forest

Just four square miles (10 square kilometers) of African rain forest can be home to about 2,250 kinds of plants and 685 kinds of animals.

Monkeys, flying squirrels, birds, bats, and tree frogs live in the forest canopy. Anteaters, snakes, wild pigs, mice, forest elephants, baboons, and gorillas are suited to life on the shady forest floor.

Forest elephants have rounded ears. Their tusks are almost straight. This keeps them from getting caught on branches and vines.

Camels are sometimes called "ships of the desert."

Across the Desert

For desert people, the most important animals are dromedary (DROM-uh-der-ee) camels. For thousands of years, these one-humped camels have carried people and goods across the desert. Dromedaries store fat in their hump. They can go without food or water for as long as a week.

Dromedaries are well adapted for the desert's heat, sandstorms, and lack of water. To keep out sand, they can either close their nostrils or leave just a small gap to breathe through. They have thick eyelashes. An extra eyelid acts like a window wiper. The eyelid is so thin that the camel can see through it when the eyelid is closed.

On the Savanna

The African savanna is home to millions of animals. They include the cheetah, which is one of the big cats, the giraffe, and the African elephant.

Cheetahs are the fastest land animals. They can sprint at 70 miles (112 kilometers) an hour. Their claws do not retract completely. Instead they dig into the ground, giving the speeding cat better grip.

Savanna elephants are the largest land animal. They use their long trunks to grip, feed, drink, smell, and spray themselves with water.

Giraffes are the tallest animal. Their long necks let them feed on leaves at the top of tall trees.

The African savanna is dotted with termite mounds. Some are 30 feet (9 meters) high.

A river hippopotamus can stay under the water without breathing for about 30 minutes.

Dangerous Times

Today, many African animals are in danger. In recent years, huge areas of savanna and rain forest have been cleared. Whole groups of animals are at risk of dying out. This is because their **environment** has changed so greatly and so rapidly. They are unable to cope with the change. Widespread hunting of endangered animals has made the problem worse.

Many African countries are taking action. They have outlawed hunting of endangered animals and have made a firm commitment to protecting Africa's wildlife.

Sounds of a Land

Like people all over the world, Africans use music and dance for all kinds of reasons and occasions. Drums, harps, lutes, thumb pianos, flutes, horns, and tambourines are among the traditional music-making instruments. Today, Western and electronic instruments are also used. Much African music now has a global reach.

Storytellers

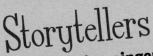

In West Africa, singers called griots (GREE-ohs) keep history alive with song stories about great events and legendary heroes.

Rebel Music

Rai (RYE) developed in Algeria. It is a mix of popular music and Bedouin music. *Rai* is used to voice opinions. Its musicians have often come into conflict with government authorities.

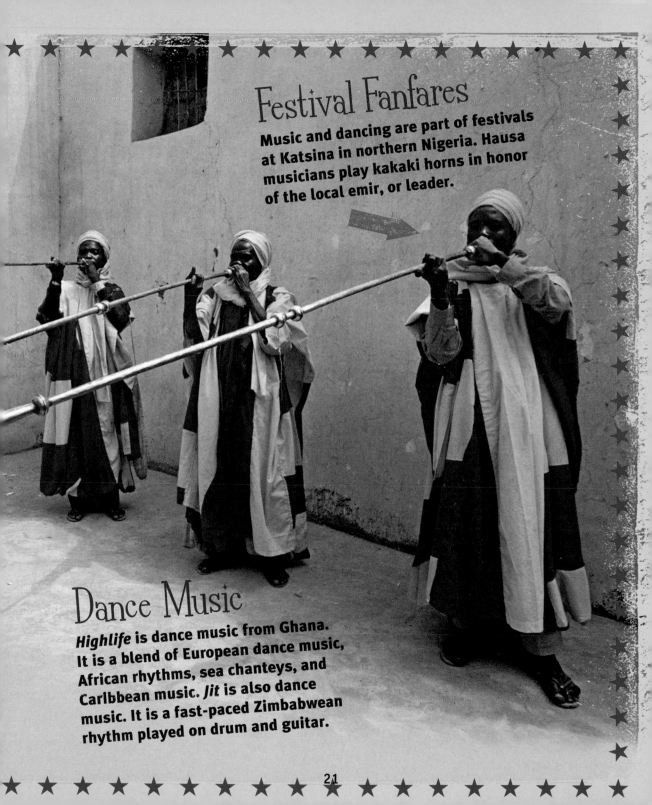

Festival Fanfares

Music and dancing are part of festivals at Katsina in northern Nigeria. Hausa musicians play kakaki horns in honor of the local emir, or leader.

Dance Music

Highlife is dance music from Ghana. It is a blend of European dance music, African rhythms, sea chanteys, and Caribbean music. *Jit* is also dance music. It is a fast-paced Zimbabwean rhythm played on drum and guitar.

These *Diictodon* fossils are about 200 million years old. They were discovered in Karoo National Park, South Africa.

CHAPTER 3

Africa Then

Africa's land is rich in resources. Gold, diamonds, and oil are abundant. But the continent's greatest treasure may be its ancient bones and **fossils**. Discoveries show that dinosaurs and the earliest **mammals** roamed Africa 200 million years ago. They also show that Africa was the likely birthplace of humans, about six million years ago.

Africa produces almost half of the world's diamonds.

Ancient Empire

Africa has produced great cultures and empires. The most famous is the Egyptian empire. It lasted for 3,000 years.

Ancient Egypt grew up in the Nile River valley 5,000 years ago. The ancient Egyptians were great scientists and artists. Many of the pyramids they built as tombs for their rulers are still standing. They are the world's largest stone structures. The Great Pyramid of Giza is built of about 200 million blocks of stone.

It took 170 men pulling on ropes to drag one block into place.

Trade Center

Great Zimbabwe

From the 1100s to the 1400s, Great Zimbabwe (zim-BAH-bweh), in southeast Africa, was a rich and powerful city. Its traders traveled as far as India and China. The city was built of stone. (*Zimbabwe* means "stone building.")

In about 1450, the city was abandoned, perhaps because its resources were used up. Archaeologists studying the ruins found bird sculptures. The modern nation of Zimbabwe has chosen a bird as its national symbol.

Two girls walk past the ruins of the stone wall that surrounded Great Zimbabwe. The wall is 36 feet (11 meters) high.

25

A Vast Continent

Much of Africa remained unexplored by outsiders until the 1400s. The land was too vast and too challenging. Then, in the early 1400s, a Chinese explorer, Zheng He (juhng huh), visited East Africa. He took a giraffe home with him. In 1488, Bartolemeu Dias, a Portuguese explorer, was the first European to sail around the Cape of Good Hope, at the southern tip of Africa. The explorers were soon followed by traders in search of gold, ivory, and slaves.

Bartolemeu Dias

The coast between Togo and Nigeria was called the Slave Coast because its main export was people.

Trade in Lives

For four centuries, European nations became wealthy trading in Africa's natural riches as well as in human beings. Between 1500 and the 1880s, more than 10 million Africans were shipped from Africa as slaves. They were transported under cruel conditions. Most were taken to the Caribbean and South America. Some were taken to what is now the United States.

Africans were packed closely together in the holds of the ships. Many died.

Land Grab

In the 1800s, European explorers mapped large areas of Africa. On the basis of those maps, countries laid claim to vast areas of Africa. The Africans had no say in the matter.

Many European nations sent white settlers to Africa to live and work in their new **colonies**. Well-armed soldiers went along to defend them. European economies soon became dependent on the riches they gained from exploiting African people and resources. By 1914, only two countries—Liberia and Ethiopia—remained free from colonial rule.

British explorer Mary Kingsley studied the peoples and animals of western Africa. She believed that the cultures of Africa should be respected.

Many European settlers tried to re-create life as it was in their home country. Some set up large farms and employed African laborers. In tropical regions, Europeans died in great numbers from malaria and other diseases. Africans died from the same diseases, as well as from diseases the settlers brought with them.

In the 1800s, people who explored Africa were treated the way movie stars are today.

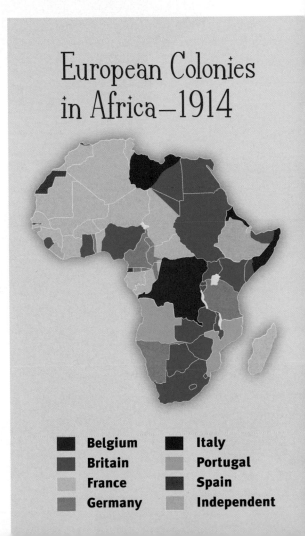

European Colonies in Africa—1914

Belgium
Britain
France
Germany
Italy
Portugal
Spain
Independent

In 2007, Ghanaians gathered to celebrate 50 years of independence.

CHAPTER 4

Free at Last!

World War II (1939–45) left many European nations weakened. Africans saw this as an opportunity to push for independence. By 1976, most African nations had won their freedom. Some managed to do so peacefully. Others had to go through violent struggles. The change was not easy for any country.

When Ghana became independent in 1957, it marked the beginning of the end of colonialism in Africa.

A Different Kind of Freedom

One of the most famous African freedom struggles occurred in South Africa. The nation became independent in 1931. But the ruling white minority refused to share power with the black majority. Instead, the government passed laws to keep blacks and whites apart.

In 1976, some black students held a protest against these laws. Police opened fire and killed 23 people. The deaths sparked riots across South Africa. More than 500 people died. The protest became known as the Soweto Uprising.

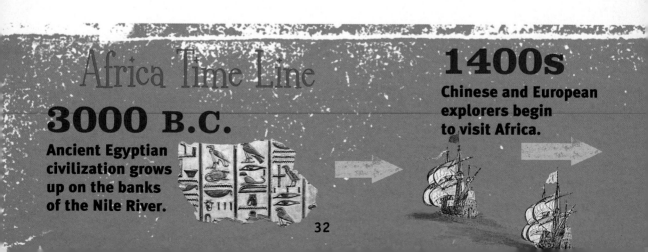

Africa Time Line

3000 B.C.
Ancient Egyptian civilization grows up on the banks of the Nile River.

1400s
Chinese and European explorers begin to visit Africa.

The Soweto killings shocked the world. Over time, South African civil rights won worldwide support. By 1991, every racist law had been withdrawn.

In 1993, two South Africans shared the Nobel Peace Prize for their efforts to bring blacks and whites together. They were' Nelson Mandela and Frederik Willem de Klerk. Mandela was a civil rights leader who had spent 26 years in prison for opposing racism. De Klerk was president of South Africa. In 1994, Nelson Mandela became South Africa's first black president.

1780s
African slave trade is at its peak.

1930– 1990
Most African colonies win their independence from European powers.

Nelson Mandela

The young men of the Wodaabe
(Wo-DAH-bay) people of western Africa
paint their faces for traditional song
and dance.

CHAPTER 5

Africa Now

The peoples of Africa are extremely varied. North of the Sahara, the people are mostly of Arab origin. South of the desert, the people are mostly black Africans. A small percentage of Africans are descendants of European settlers. Many Africans speak several languages.

In 2005, Ellen Johnson-Sirleaf became president of Liberia. She was the first elected woman head of state in Africa. →

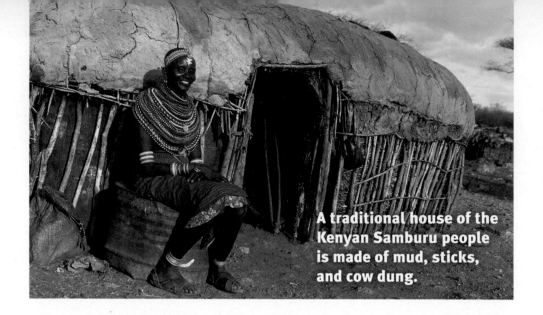

A traditional house of the Kenyan Samburu people is made of mud, sticks, and cow dung.

Country Life

Only four out of ten Africans live in cities. Most are farmers or herders in the countryside. Some Africans follow ways of life that have changed little since ancient times.

Many Africans still live in traditional houses. Some homes are made of mud walls topped with metal sheets. The thick mud helps keep the house cool. Others have roofs made of thick grass. In the desert, many families live in tents.

Rising to the Challenge

Africans face many challenges. **Life expectancy** in some countries is still low. In Zambia, it is only 35 years. Malaria is the leading cause of death in Africa. It is caused by a bite from an infected mosquito. Other diseases, and wars in some areas, also cause great suffering.

Droughts are common in parts of Africa. When they occur, crops die. Animals and people are in danger of starving. One cause of drought is loss of trees. For 30 years, Kenyan environmentalist Dr. Wangari Maathai has encouraged Africans to plant trees. In Kenya alone, 30 million trees have been planted.

Dr. Maathai planting a tree

In South Africa, Ndebele women paint their houses in colorful geometric designs.

Art in Life

Much African art is made to be used as well as admired. Objects such as bowls, chairs, and even houses are things of beauty. Amazing masks and headdresses play a key role in religious events.

Like artists all over the world, many Africans produce art that suits their way of life. Herders often make art that can be easily carried, such as baskets. **Nomads** are known for their body painting and jewelry. Wood carving is common among forest dwellers.

People of the Savanna

The Maasai of East Africa are herders. Although less land for grazing is available to them today, they are still partly nomadic. They move with the seasons as they look for grass and water for their livestock.

The Maasai treasure their cattle. Cattle are their main source of food, milk, wealth, and importance. The Maasai believe that all cattle were created specially for them.

There are 30 Maasai words for cattle. Some refer to the color or the shape of the horns.

Mbuti adults average only four and a half feet (1.3 meters) in height.

Mbuti houses are a beehive-shaped frame of sticks covered with leaves. They can be built very quickly.

People of the Rain Forest

The Mbuti (im-BOO-tee) have lived in the Ituri rain forest in Democratic Republic of Congo for more than 4,000 years. The forest is sacred to them. At times of celebration, they sing songs to it.

Mbuti houses are simple because they are not permanent homes. The people move camp every month or so, following their food supply. They do not cultivate their food. They eat nuts and berries from the forest, and hunt mammals.

Blue Men

The Tuareg are one of the African groups who call the desert their home. They are nomads who live in the Sahara.

Tuareg men wear a cloth around their heads and cover their faces in front of strangers and women. They are called "Blue Men" because of their blue clothing. Boys plait their hair and grease it with butter to protect it from the sun. At eighteen, they receive a head cloth and veil.

Camels are very precious to the Tuareg. They use them for food, clothing, and transport. White camels are the most valuable because they are quite rare.

Sharing Cultures

Some African clothing is known for its bold colors and designs. Kente (KEN-tay) cloth is probably the most famous African fabric. Kente patterns were created in the twelfth century by the Ashanti people of West Africa. Kente was woven for Ashanti royalty.

Today, kente cloth has come to symbolize African pride and unity. It is worn by Africans everywhere for weddings, baby-namings, and other special events. ★

An Ashanti boy dressed in kente cloth holds a copy of the golden Ashanti stool. The stool is a symbol of the spirit of the Ashanti people.